THE KOREAN MARTIAL ART OF SELF DEFENSE

HAP KI DO
합기도

KI-BON-GI-SOOL
기본기술

By Master Choe

©Copyright 1998 HUI S CHOE

ISBN 0-9668254-0-3

Published by HUI S CHOE

Cover and technique photos by Clememte
Cover and book design by Chito - Westco Mkt., Inc.

10 9 8 7 6 5 4 3 2

WORLD
HAP KI DO

Master Choe

FOREWORD

I have been training in Martial Arts since I was 6 years old. My mother held my hand and took me to enroll in a Tae Kwon Do School near my home in Seoul, Korea. The Dojang was where I met Master Ko on that first day, I remember being afraid of him.

At the school I also saw a lot of excellent pictures of people and Master Ko doing Tae Kwon Do. These pictures gave me a strong motivation to learn this style of Martial Arts.

Training in Tae Kwon Do for many years made me fall in love with Martial Arts. I wanted to learn other styles of Martial Arts. I found a Hap Ki Do School located near my middle school. There, I worked hard to learn Hap Ki Do from Grandmaster Yoon, instructors and black belts. After years of learning, I tested for my black belt with six other students. Even though I passed, I had the lowest grade. I was so disappointed, because I worked so hard to learn. I also wanted to stop practicing Hap Ki Do.

During this time I met Kim and Ma who already were black belts. They asked me if I wanted to join them in practicing Martial Arts in the mountain. I agreed and we dedicated ourselves to learning as many Martial Arts as we could. Unfortunately, finding a book on Hap Ki Do was very hard. The reason being is that Hap Ki Do at that time was a secret Martial Art. It was taught from one person to the other without the help of literature.

I have been collecting books on Martial Arts for some time now. Here in the United States there are only a very few Hap Ki Do books written. This is my reason for writing this Hap Ki Do book for beginners who wish to learn this Martial Art. My hope is through the natural form of progress somebody else will write another book on Hap Ki Do. This will keep this Martial Art progressing.

I would like to take this time to thank all my students who contributed in making this book. I would also like to thank all the Master Instructors in Washington State.

> \- Master H. S. Choe
> World Hap Ki Do (Spanaway, WA)

I have known Master Choe since 1989. Master Choe has demonstrated a great sense of love and devotion in the Martial Art of Hap Ki Do. He has dedicated his life in not only mastering this art form, but in passing it on to all who would be interested in learning it.

The instructional video tapes and booklets that he has put out have been fantastic, but the accomplishment of this book has been a great achievement to his dedication and devotion to Hap Ki Do. I am very proud of him and truly hope that others will appreciate this book.

> \- Grandmaster Y.H. Lee
> World Tae Kwon Do (Auburn, WA)

TABLE OF CONTENTS

HISTORY OF HAP KI DO

I t should be first understood that a Martial Art is not invented or created by any one person. Techniques are developed by many over a great number of years. Just as Wrestling, Boxing, and Fencing are unique to the western world, Martial Arts have been developed through a long history of Asian Countries.

During the Three Kingdom Era (SAM-KUK-SHI-DAE) (From 57 B.C. to 668 A.D.) Three Kingdoms competed on the Korean peninsula: KO-GU-RYO (37 B.C.) in the North, PAEK-JAB (18 B.C.) in the South West, and SHILLA (57 B.C.) in the South East. Martial Arts techniques much like those of modern day HAP-KI-DO were introduced to ancient Korea with the introduction of Buddhism in KO-GU-RYO approximately 372 A.D. Evidence of the existence of HAP-KI-DO techniques during the Three Kingdom Era can be found in many of the ancient wall and cave paintings and sculptures from that period of time.

During the SHILLA (57 B.C. to 660 A.D.) and the United SHILLA Kingdom (676 A.D. to 935 A.D.) Each King gathered about him an elite group of young Knights, the HWA-RANG (Flowering Youth) WARRIORS, who were highly disciplined, adhered to a strict code of ethics and were extremely proficient in the Martial Arts. These Warriors who were to train the future national leaders were taught HAP-KI-DO techniques for their physical fitness, mental discipline and Self-Defense.

The SHILLA Kingdom was over turned in 935 A.D. by the Dynasty of KO-RYO, from which the name "Korea" was derived. During the KO-RYO Dynasty (918 A.D.-1392 A.D.) Buddhism was the state religion and greatly influenced politics and administrations as well as Martial Arts. Many Kings, including King EYI-JONG, and King CHOONG-HEI, brought HAP-KI-DO experts into the palace to perform demonstrations of the Martial Arts. This was the beginning of HAP-KI-DO as a Royal Martial Art.

In the history of HAP-KI-DO, a Monk Grandmaster SU-SAN taught HAP-Kl-DO to the Monks who were successful in repelling the Japanese invaders during the IN-JIN-WAE-RAN Invasion. This was a prime example of HAP-KI-DO applied on a grand scale.

In the new CHO-SON Dynasty (1392-1910) or YI Dynasty as it is often called, the collapse of Buddhism came about and its subsequent replacement by Confucianism ... which respects scholarly disciplines and looks down upon physical force or Martial Arts, brought about the down fall of Martial Arts. Painting, sculpting, and writing replaced the art of fighting. The country progressively took on an anti-militaristic temperament. By the end of the nineteenth century, Martial Arts had come to be looked down upon by the Korean citizen, if not completely banned in many regions. HAP-KI-DO barely maintained it's continuation through individual Masters, Buddhist Monks and Royal families, practicing the arts in seclusion. In an attempt to prevent the complete loss of the fighting arts, King JUNG-JO ordered his general, LEE, DUK-MOO to compile a book of all the known Martial Art techniques. The book known as MOO-YAE-DO-BO-TONG-JI has many detailed examples of HAP-Kl-DO techniques recorded within it's pages.

The CHO-SON Dynasty was brought down by the Japanese in 1910. From 1910 to 1945 Korea was ruled by the Japanese. Under Japanese rule all civil liberties were revoked. The Japanese closed many private schools and established their own public schools designed to assimilate Korean youth into the Japanese culture, omitting Korean language and history and stressing Japan's instead. The Martial Arts again suffered since the occupying Japanese would not even allow Korean sports let alone Korean Martial Arts to be practiced. But as before those dedicated few continued to practice, quietly defying there invading rulers.

In 1945 after Korea regained control of their country, the Martial Arts once again gained popularity in this defense hungry nation. HAP-KI-DO was reintroduced by the man given the title of founder or father of modern day HAP-KI-DO, CHOI,YONG-SOOL. Before his death in 1987 Supreme Grandmaster CHOI taught all the HAP-KI-DO techniques to a few outstanding students, who in turn took on the task of popularizing HAP-KI-DO in modern Korea. Today, one cannot find a single city in Korea without HAP-KI-DO Schools. All the Government organizations, all the Military academies and special Military units have HAP-KI-DO Instructors and practitioners totaling over one million already.

Among foreign Countries such as the USA, Germany, Canada, Spain, Brazil, Argentina, Mexico, China, and France, there is a solid foundation of HAP-KI-DO Schools that is continuing through the unending dedication of the HAP-KI-DO Masters throughout the World.

WHAT IS HAP KI DO?

HAP-Kl-DO: It is a discipline of coordination, a way of strengthening the mind and body, of fusing the individuals physical and mental powers so that he or she will emerge as a more fully integrated human being. The word in fact means; Method or Way (DO) for the Coordination Harmony (HAP) of Mental Energy or Spirit (KI). One should always try to avoid violence, but if someone grabs you, attempts to strike you, or physically assaults you in any way, it has escalated beyond words, and you are left with the only option which is to defend. The Korean Art of Self-Defense, HAP-Kl-DO is considered a "soft" style of Martial Art, as opposed to "hard" styles that practice the use of force against force, making the outcome a simple matter of size and strength. The HAP-Kl-DO practitioner diverts or suppresses an attackers flow of energy peacefully, this diversion allows him to use the attackers power against himself leading to the attackers defeat. Through the use of pressure on certain skeletal joints and pressure points, very little strength is needed to overcome an opponent.

HAP-KI-DO not only redirects the attack, but turns it back against the attacker and follows through with offensive techniques which may control his violence or render him incapable of further antagonistic actions. The HAP-KI-DO practitioner is in complete control of the confrontation defusing the aggression without the need for uncontrolled damage as seen in many "hard" styles.

HAP-KI-DO provides complete physical conditioning which improves balance, posture, flexibility, timing, quickness, muscle tone, joint strength, and most importantly, confidence through physical and mental discipline.

The immediate aim of HAP-KI-DO is of course the welfare of the one practicing it. Not only will skills in Self-Defense be attained, but more importantly will be the focus on an individuals character development. A well rounded personality can be realized only if the spirit is right. Courtesy, Respect, Modesty, Loyalty, Generosity and Dedication are not only the source, but also the rewards of HAP-KI-DO!

JOON-BI-WOON-DONG
EXERCISE

ADVANCE EXERCISES PUSH-UPS

Knuckle Push-Ups
These are intended to develop strength while conditioning the knuckles. Start out on softer surfaces first then work your way toward harder surfaces. Cement being the ultimate surface. Remember that in punching you will be breaking primarily with the first two knuckles so concentrate the stress of the push-ups against these two knuckles

Fingertip Push-Ups
These push-ups are intended to strengthen your fingers and hands so you can squeeze pressure point areas harder. You will notice that there is considerable difference between the stress placed on hand that are only slightly curled and the discomfort experienced when you are really high up on the tips of your fingers. Experiment with different elevations and force yourself to move slowly. Concentrations on good form and keeping your shoulder blades down when you feel it easy to push-up. Do push-ups with four fingers then three, then two, and finally one.

ADVANCE EXERCISES SIT-UPS

Sit-ups
Close your fingers together and put it behind your neck. Partner holds your legs tightly. Raise up your body towards your legs and close up your elbows together. Go back down slowly.

Reverse Sit-ups
Partner sits on your legs and holding your ankle. Put your hands together on your lower back. Raise up your head slowly as high as you can. Go back down slowly and exhale.

ADVANCE EXERCISES PUSH-UPS

With a handstand position, your partner holds your ankles tightly with both hands. Go down slowly and go back up to full extension. Focus your eyes on the mat to keep your balance.

JOINTS EXERCISE

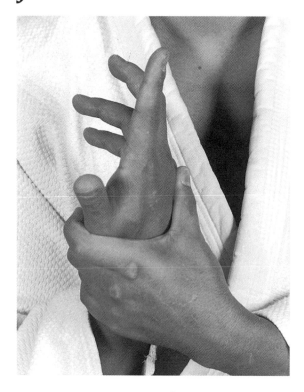

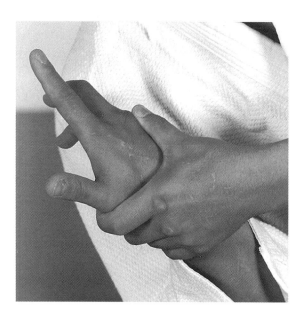

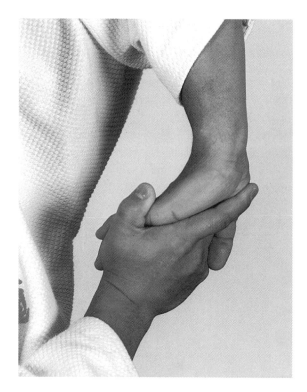

Boo-Chae Exercise

Raise your right hand to chest level with palm facing your chest. With your left hand, grab the back of the right hand with your fingers around the base of the right thumb and your left thumb between the knuckle and below your ring finger and middle finger. With the left hand and thumb, twist the right hand towards the right while pushing down. You should feel a slight pain.

Yung-Hang Exercise

With the left hand, palm facing down, point fingers towards the body. Elbow should be facing up and away from body. This position should feel awkward. Take the right hand with palm facing up and grasp left hand (locking hands together). With hand locked together, use right hand to apply pressure on the left hand and wrist. You should feel a slight pain in the left wrist. Elbow should be pointed towards the ceiling.

JOINTS EXERCISE

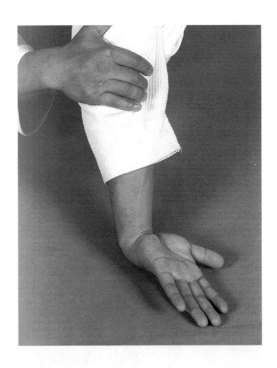

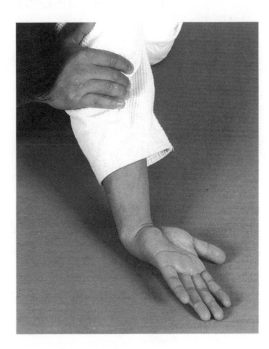

Hei-Jun Exercise

Grab the back of your right hand with your left hand. The left thumb circles your right thumb. Bring both hands up close to your chest keeping your elbows down while flexing and stretching your right wrist inward until your fingers on your right hand touch your right forearm if possible. Some pain may be experienced at first until your wrist ligaments develop the necessary strength and elasticity

Pal-Kum-Chi Exercise

Straight arm out on the mat with the elbow and the palm of your hand facing up. The palm of your other hand is pressing on your elbow.

DAN-JUN BREATHING

DAN-JUN-HO-HUP, unique to the art of HAP-KI-DO, are special breathing exercises that have been developed and practiced for over 2,000 years in Korea. Very simply stated, DAN-JUN breathing means "abdominal breathing". By improving ones breathing using DAN-JUN breathing a person can increase their physical and mental health. DAN-JUN breathing will help to increase your lung capacity allowing you to breath much easier during training, sparing or actual combat.

DAN-JUN-HO-HUP is important in HAP-KI-DO because it is believed to be a source of great inner power. We call this inner power "KI". In HAP-KI-DO, physical power is called "WAE-KI" while mental power is called "NAE-KI". HAP-KI-DO, meaning the Art, Method or Way (DO) for the Coordination/Harmony (HAP) of Mental energy/Power (KI), seeks to unite these powers.

To maintain good mental and physical health one must maintain the balance between NAE-KI and WAE-KI. WAE-KI (outer power) can be seen and measured. WAE-KI is seen when a person walks, runs, jumps, lifts, pushes, etc. We develop WAE-KI in our daily practice through our exercises, kicking, and HO-SHIN-SOOL.

NAE-KI is what we usually refer to as "KI", This KI power is inner or mental power. NAE-KI is power of the spirit and patience. We cannot see this power, but unlike WAE-KI, NAE-KI is limitless. Examples of NAE-KI occurring spontaneously, without prior training are the many documented cases of persons who, under extreme circumstances of fear or stress, lift or move an object which would normally require the strength of ten people, such as a mother lifting a car under which her child is trapped. It is this power we seek to gain control over.

NAE-KI is fully developed with DAN-JUN breathing exercises. Most people breath with their chest while DAN-JUN breathing is done with the abdomen (as a baby does naturally). The DAN-JUN area, or seat of this power is located one to three inches below the navel, It is comprised of three points: KI-HAE, located one inch below the navel; KWAN-WON, two inches below the navel; and SUK-MAN, three inches below the navel. In the Oriental Medical System this area is often called KI-HYA. Which means "power like the ocean". This point is considered to be the "center" of the human body where all power and energy comes from. DAN-JUN-HO-HOP creates and develops power, focuses power and conserves power. In Korean philosophy the universe is very large while the human body is very small, KI flows from the large universe, which is very strong with KI, to the small human body. It is DAN-JUN-HO-HUP that enables the KI from the universe to flow into the human body.

In HAP-KI-DO there are many types of DAN-JUN breathing exercises. We will concentrate on the basic and the crucial ones for the development of HAP-KI-DO.

1. Put your fist on your belt, and open your legs shoulder width.

2. As you raise your hands and your heels, inhale slowly, and stop at your eyebrows. Hold your breath.

3. Turn your hands over and open your fingers, bend your knees, lower your hands to your belt and exhale.

1. Hands on the side of your belt. With a ready stance. Inhale slowly through your nose.

2. Hold your breath and bend your knees, start raising your hands slowly.

3. When you raise your hand at shoulder level, exhale and return to first position.

KI-HAP

An enigma to most beginner students. They fail to understand why they are taught to "yell" at certain times during their training sessions. HAP-KI-DO seeks to coordinate mental and physical power, making a yelling sound helps unite the mind and body toward the action being performed.

You will develop your own style of KI-HAP over time and probably change it several times. Don't get caught up in trying to say "KI-HAP" when performing the KI-HAP, simply make a loud noise. Which serves to not only help facilitate the joining of the mind and body, but is a great stress reliever as well.

A good KI-HAP is developed and summoned from the lower abdomen (DAN-JUN) which is the center of everyone's power or energy. You must remember that KI-HAP and concentration go hand in hand. Both of these will help the Martial Artist bring their mind, body and spirit together for the propose of making their actions strong, quick, and precise. When KI-HAP and concentration are practiced faithfully, precise techniques, power and better overall physical conditioning can be achieved.

The sun's warm rays can tan the skin in several hours, but if you intensify the heat by using a magnifying glass you will be burned severely. In the same manner the developed KI-HAP will greatly magnify your power.

BREAKFALLS (NAK-BUP)

Proper, safe falling is essential to the practice of HAP-KI-DO techniques. Without NAK-BUP practice and use during technique training, your HO-SHIN-SOOL techniques will not progress properly. If HAP-KI-DO is going to be learned, NAK-BUP has to be mastered. The two, HAP-KI-DO and NAK-BUP, are inseparable. Most people don't understand the correct way or appropriate time to fall. Inadequate NAK-BUP eventually creates problems with techniques resulting in injuries. Even though a person may appear strong, if he mistakenly falls an injury may occur easily, So, one must concentrate at all times during practice and pay attention to breakfalling. Through the use of a proper falling surface (mats) and proper NAK-BUP training, joint-locking and throwing can be done with great speed and power without harm. The body must be kept loose and relaxed while falling.

NAK-BUP actually massages the whole body, increases circulation, and warms the body. The stiffness of old age can be avoided by the practice of NAK-BUP. Improper NAK-BUP however, can and will lead to injury, so it is essential that you maintain complete concentration in what you are doing during practice. Listen carefully to your master instructor's instructions and learn the proper method of NAK-BUP so you can become proficient in this very important skill.

You will learn several variations of NAK-BUP to prevent injury no matter what direction you fall. There is: Forward drop breakfalls, or JUHN-BAHNG NAK-BUP. Backward breakfalls, or HOO-BAHNG NAK-BUP. Basic forward breakfalls, or simply HEI-JUN NAK-BUP. Jumping or diving breakfalls, or JAHNG-AYE-MOOL NAK-BUP. And at the advanced levels the free-fall (no hands) breakfalls, KONG-JOONG HEI-JUN NAK-BUP.

1. Stand with your feet twelve to sixteen inches apart, with your toes pointing outward at a 45 degree angle. Now squat down with your hips slightly raised and with your knees pointing in the same direction as your toes. Place your hands on the mat, making a 90 degree triangle

2. Push off with your left foot, allowing the right to come up naturally. Keep your head away from the mat.

3. Roll along the line of your right arm and across the back of your shoulders. Keep your head bent and watching your belt.

4. You will fall on your left side hitting the mat hard with the full left arm, your left leg bend a little bit and your right leg and foot parallel with and slightly to the rear of the left.

KI-BON-SOOL
기 본 술

BOO-CHAE
부 채

Boo-Chae 1

1. As your opponent grabs your right wrist, open your hand and spread your fingers, loosening his grip.

2. Move towards him. Grab his right hand with your left hand, keeping your fingers on top. Rotate your hand counterclockwise

3. Place both of your thumbs on the back of his hand. Twist the wrist while stepping back with your left leg. (Ban-Hei-Jun step)

4. Forcing him to the ground, continue circular motion with the wrist while placing your right knee behind his elbow.

Boo-Chae 2 (Yock-Boo-Chae)

1. When your opponent grabs your left wrist with his right hand, spread your fingers loosening his grip.

2. Turn your hand counterclockwise with your palm facing up. With your right hand grab his hand underneath

3. Use your right hand to twist his hand while stepping back with your left foot (Ban-Hei-Jun step) take him down to the ground.

4. Place your right knee on his shoulder while twisting his wrist.

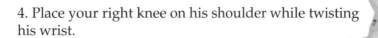

23

Boo-Chae 3 (Yock-Boo-Chae)

1. As your opponent grabs both of your wrists, you move one step forward with your right foot.

2. Move your left hand counter-clockwise with your palm facing you. With your right hand, reach underneath and grab the back of his hand.

3. Use your right hand to twist his hand while stepping back with your left foot (Ban-Hei-Jun step) taking him to the ground.

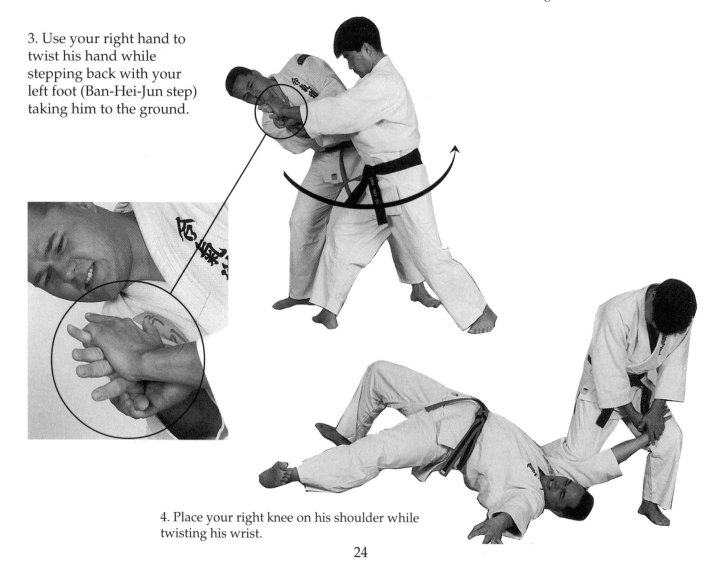

4. Place your right knee on his shoulder while twisting his wrist.

24

Boo-Chae 4

1. When your opponent grabs your right wrist with both hands.

2. Short step forward while grabbing his right wrist with your left hand.

3. Rotate your right arm counter clockwise to free your right hand.

4. Grab the back of his right hand with both your hands. Turning your body 180 degrees, take him down to the mat.

5. Put your right knee on his right shoulder while twisting his arm counter clockwise.

Boo-Chae 5

1. As your opponent stands behind you grabbing both of your wrists.

2. Step forward with your left foot as you twist your hips to the right.

(A) Grab on the back of his hand above with your right hand. Make a fist with your left hand and rotate it to free your hand from his grip.

(A)

5. Ma-Moo-Ri (Finishing Move): Put your left knee on his left shoulder blade while pressing his neck with your left thumb.

4. Turn clockwise and grab his hand with your left hand. Hold on to his hand with both hands. Twist his hand and take him to the mat.

3. Kick his body with your right side kick

Boo-Chae 6

1. Your opponent grabs your sleeves from behind you

2. Step forward and around with your left foot while pulling up and around

3. As you come under with your right arm, grab the back of his right hand with your left hand.

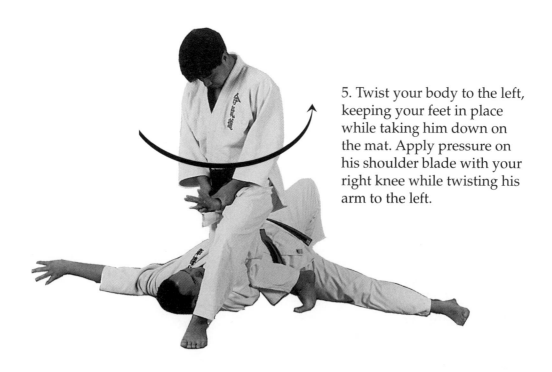

5. Twist your body to the left, keeping your feet in place while taking him down on the mat. Apply pressure on his shoulder blade with your right knee while twisting his arm to the left.

4. Hold on to his hand with both of your hands

Boo-Chae 7

1. Your opponent grabs your right shoulder and wrist from behind.

2. Step forward with your left foot while bending your right elbow.

3. Reach around with your left hand grabbing the back of his right hand.

6. Place your right knee on his shoulder blade while twisting his hand counter clockwise.

5. While holding his right hand, step around with your left foot. Twisting his wrist, take him down to the mat.

4. Rotate your right arm counter clockwise to free your right hand. With your right, grab the back of his right hand.

31

Boo-Chae 8

1. Assume a ready position. As your opponent strikes with his right fist, step to the left with your left foot and block his fist with your left forearm. Then grab the back of his right hand with your left hand.

2. Take your right hand and grab his hand while holding on with your left hand.

3. Step forward with your right foot and rotate to the left (360 degrees) while twisting his hand. Take him down to the mat.

Boo-Chae 9

1. Assume a ready position.

2. As he moves forward to stab, step to your left side. You block and grab the back of his right hand with both of your hands.

3. Step forward with your left foot a little bit and twist his right hand.

4. Turn your body (360 degrees) and press his hand down to the mat.

* Keypoint : You have to press his hand as you turn your body.

Boo-Chae 10

1. Assume a fighting stance

2. As your opponent strikes to the head, step to the left side, grab the back of his right hand with your left hand and then grab underneath with your right hand.

3. Step forward with your left foot while twisting his right hand.

4. As you step forward with your right foot, press his right hand down to the mat.

Boo-Chae 11

1. Assume a fighting stance — As your opponent moves to strike

2. Step to the left side (45 degrees) with your left foot and grab his right hand with both of your hands.

2. Reverse view.

3. Turn your body (180 degrees) while you pull his arm.

3. Reverse view.

4. Step forward deeply with your right foot.

4. Reverse View

5. As you step with your left foot, rotate your body (180 degrees) and press his hand down to the mat.

5. Reverse View

HEI-JUN
회전

Hei-Jun 1

1. As your opponent grabs you with his right hand, open your right hand.

2. Deep step forward with your right foot and grab the back of his right hand with your left hand.

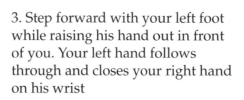

3. Step forward with your left foot while raising his hand out in front of you. Your left hand follows through and closes your right hand on his wrist

6. Pressure his right elbow with your left hand and drive it into the mat.

5. Pull his wrist to the mat and place your right knee against his chest.

4. While pivoting around (180 degrees) clockwise duck underneath his arm, pull his wrist to the mat.

Hei-Jun 2

1. As your opponent grabs your left wrist with his right hand, open your left hand.

2. Deep step with your right foot (45 degrees to the right) and grab his right wrist with your right hand.

3. While pivoting around clockwise duck underneath his arm, pull his wrist to the mat.

4. Step forward with your left foot. As you throw him to the mat, place your left hand on his right elbow and press down.

Hei-Jun 3

1. As your opponent grabs both of your wrists, open both of your hands.

2. Deep step with your right foot (45 degrees to the right) and grab his right wrist with your right hand.

3. Step forward with your left foot while raising his hand out in front of you.

4. While pivoting around clockwise duck underneath his arm, Step forward with your right foot and pull his wrist to the mat.

5. Grab his right elbow with your left hand and drive it into the mat.

Hei-Jun 4

1. While your opponent grabs your right wrist with both of his hands, open your hand. (spread your fingers)

2. Deep step with your right foot (45 degrees to the right) and grab the back of his right hand with your left hand.

3. Step forward with your left foot while raising his hand out in front of you.

4. While pivoting around clockwise duck underneath his arm, Step forward with your right foot and pull his wrist to the mat.

Hei-Jun 5

1. As your opponent grabs both of your elbows from behind with both of his hands, open your hands. (spread your fingers)

2. Deep step with your left foot and raise your left hand up, and out in front of you.

3. While pivoting around clockwise (180 degrees), grab his right wrist with your left hand.

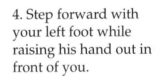

4. Step forward with your left foot while raising his hand out in front of you.

5. While pivoting around clockwise duck underneath his arm, Step forward with your right foot and pull his wrist to the mat.

Hei-Jun 6

1. As your opponent grabs both of your wrists from behind with both of his hands, open your hands. (spread your fingers)

2. Deep step with your left foot and raise your left hand up, and out in front of you.

3. While pivoting around clockwise (180 degrees), grab his right wrist with your right hand.

6. While pivoting around clockwise duck underneath his arm, Step forward with your right foot and pull his wrist to the mat.

5. Step forward with your left foot while raising his hand out in front of you.

4. Reach forward with your left hand and grab his right wrist.

Hei-Jun 7

1. Assume a fight stance

2. As your opponent lunges with a knife, back step with your left foot and grab his hand with both of your hands. In a sliding motion, push the knife away from your body.

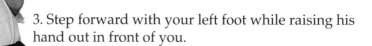

3. Step forward with your left foot while raising his hand out in front of you.

4. While pivoting around clockwise duck underneath his arm. Step forward with your right foot and pull his wrist to the mat. Then take away his knife.

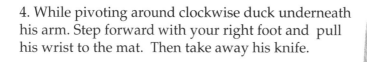

Hei-Jun 8

1. As your opponent places a gun to your forehead.

2. Deep step with your right foot, block the gun away with your left hand and grab his wrist. Then strike his body with your right fist.

3. Keeping the gun pointed away from you, bring it between you and him, and grab his right wrist with your right hand.

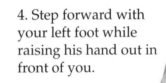

4. Step forward with your left foot while raising his hand out in front of you.

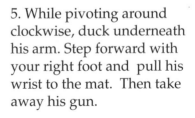

5. While pivoting around clockwise, duck underneath his arm. Step forward with your right foot and pull his wrist to the mat. Then take away his gun.

Hei-Jun 9

1. Assume a fight stance

2. Deep step with your left foot, block the long stick with your left hand as you grab his long stick with your right hand.

3. Step forward to the left side with your right foot, and rotate his long stick.

5. Then place the long stick on his neck.

4. Press down his long stick over his shoulder

49

Hei-Jun 10 (Yock-Hei-Jun)

1. As your opponent grabs your left wrist , open your hand (spread your fingers).

2. Step behind him with your right foot while grabbing his right wrist with your right hand.

3. Then raise his arm out in front of you.

5. Step forward with your right foot and pull his wrist to the mat.

4. While pivoting around clockwise duck underneath his arm.

Hei-Jun 11

1. As your opponent punches you with his right fist, block his punch with your left hand. Then grab his right wrist.

2. Deep step with your right foot and swing his arm between you. Then grab his wrist with your right hand.

3. While pivoting around clockwise (180 degrees), pull his wrist to the mat.

Hei-Jun 12

1. When your opponent grabs your right wrist with his right hand, open your hand. Grasp the back of his hand with your left hand.

2. Take a 45 degrees step forward with your right foot. At the same time raise his arm.

5. Once you have him on the mat, place your right foot under his right shoulder.

4. Stepping forward with your right foot, throw him to the mat maintaining a firm grip on his hand.

3. Deep step forward with your left foot. With his extended arm out stretched, pivot around.

6. While holding his right hand in Boo-Chae position, step over his head with your left foot.

7. Lie down on your back. Trap his arm between your knees and squeeze tightly.

8. With his arm stretched out, pull his wrist toward your chest. As you bend his elbow, choke his neck with your left foot.

Master Choe

YUN-HANG
연 행

YUNG-HANG 1

1. When your opponent grabs your right wrist with his right hand, open your hand (spread your fingers)

2. With your left hand grab his right wrist. Take a deep step with your left foot.

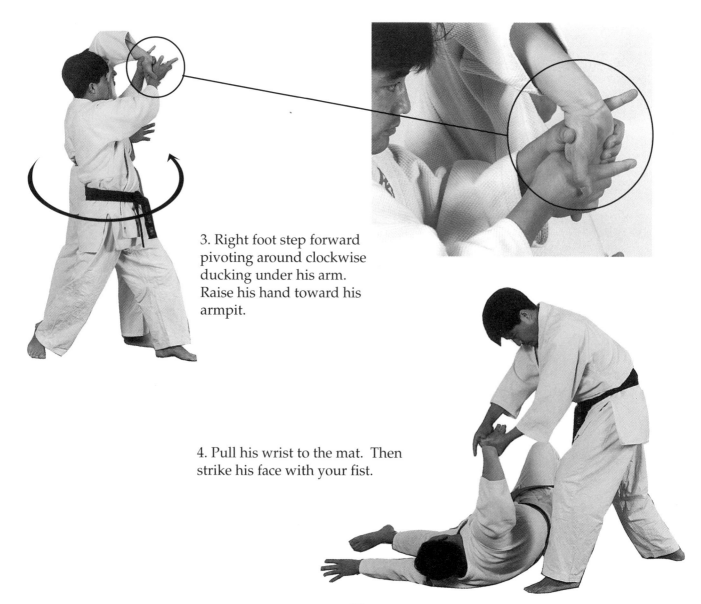

3. Right foot step forward pivoting around clockwise ducking under his arm. Raise his hand toward his armpit.

4. Pull his wrist to the mat. Then strike his face with your fist.

YUNG-HANG 2

1. When your opponent grabs your left wrist with his right hand, open your hand. (spread your fingers)

2. Grab his right hand with your right hand. At the same time take a short sliding step with your left foot.

3. Take a deep step forward with your right foot. As you raise his hand toward his armpit, ducking under pivoting 180 degrees. Move your left foot back one more step.

4. Taking a deep step forward with your left foot forward, bring his arm toward the mat.

YUNG-HANG 3

1. When your opponent grabs your right wrist with both of his hands,

2. With your left hand grab his right wrist. Take a deep step with your left foot.

3. Take a deep step with your right foot. As you raise his hand toward his armpit, duck underneath pivoting 180 degrees. (fingers toward you.)

4. While holding his wrist with your left hand, grab his fingers with your right hand.

7. Place your right knee on the mat and pull his fingers up towards you.

6. Pivoting your body around, pull his arm over and down toward the mat.

5. Taking a step back with your left foot, place your left hand on his elbow.

YUNG-HANG 4

1. When your opponent grabs your left sleeve with his right hand.

2. With your right hand grab his right hand as you step to the left 45 degrees with your left foot.

3. Take a deep step with your right foot. As you raise his hand toward his armpit, ducking under and pivoting 180 degrees.

6. Take him to the mat and push down on his elbow with your left hand.

5. As you rotate your body pull his arm over and toward the mat.

4. Take a step back with your left foot place your left hand on his right elbow.

YUNG-HANG 5

1. As your opponent punches you with his right fist, step to the left 45 degrees with your left foot and block with your right hand.

2. Grab his right wrist with both hands and raise his arm up. * Extending your index fingers to get more power (Ki)

3. Duck as you pivot around bringing his arm over your shoulder.

6. As you turn your body 180 degrees, pull him down to the mat maintaining press on his wrist.

5. Place your left hand on his right elbow.

4. Taking a step back with your left foot, raise his hand toward his armpit.

YUNG-HANG 6

1. As your opponent places a gun to your forehead.

2. Take a step to the left 45 degrees with your left foot as you grab his wrist in a fast upward motion.

3. Guide his arm down and around in a circular motion. Make sure you keep the gun pointed away from you through out the technique.

6. Taking a deep step forward with your left foot, pull his arm in a large circular motion toward the mat.

5. As you step forward with your right foot, turn your body 180 degrees, and raise his arm using pressure applied to his wrist.

4. Continue bringing the gun between you and him.

YUNG-HANG 7

1. Assume a fight stance.

2. As he stabs you with his knife, step backward with your left foot, and grab his wrist with a downward motion.

3. Take a step forward with your left foot and bring his arm up in a circular motion.

5. Taking a deep step forward with your left foot, pull his arm in a large circular motion toward the mat.

4. Stepping through with your right foot duck under his arm and pivot your body 180 degrees.

Master Choe

PAL-KUM-CHI

팔꿈치

Pal-Kum-Chi 1

1. When your opponent grabs your right wrist with his right hand,

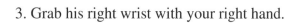

2. Turn your right hand over his right wrist in a circular motion.

3. Grab his right wrist with your right hand.

6. Finish by kneeling on the back of his shoulder with your left knee and applying constant pressure to the elbow joint with your left hand.

5. Step back with your right foot and turn your body 180 degrees, Press down on his elbow joint and push him down to the mat.

4. Step forward with your left foot. Place your left hand on his right elbow.

Pal-Kum-Chi 2

1. As your opponent grabs both of your wrists with both of his hands

2. Rotate your left hand over the top of his right wrist. Then grab the backside of his right hand.

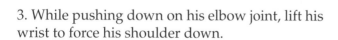

3. While pushing down on his elbow joint, lift his wrist to force his shoulder down.

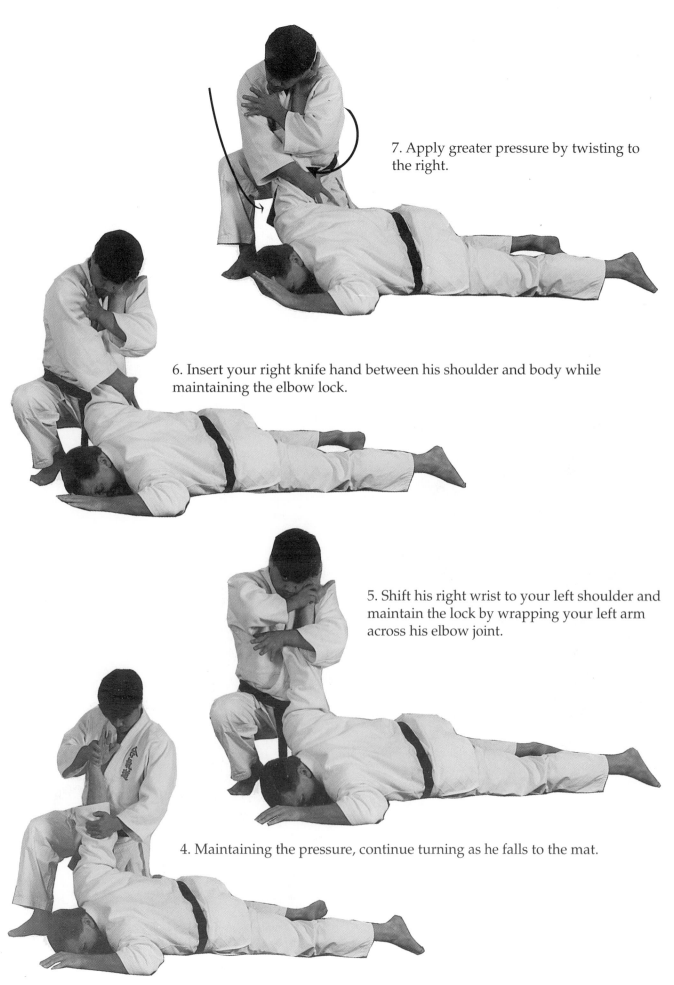

7. Apply greater pressure by twisting to the right.

6. Insert your right knife hand between his shoulder and body while maintaining the elbow lock.

5. Shift his right wrist to your left shoulder and maintain the lock by wrapping your left arm across his elbow joint.

4. Maintaining the pressure, continue turning as he falls to the mat.

Pal-Kum-Chi 3

1. As your opponent grabs your right wrist with both of his hands

2. Rotate your right hand over the top of his right wrist and step forward with your right foot.

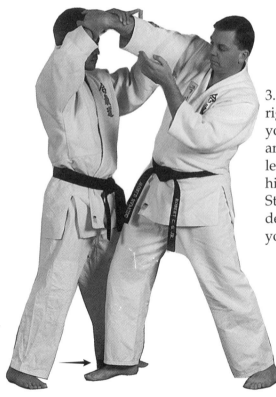

3. Grab his right wrist with your right hand and place your left hand on his elbow joint. Step forward deeply with your left foot.

4. Turn your hips and bring his arm down in a spiral until he completely loses his balance.

Pal-Kum-Chi 4

1. As your opponent grabs your left collar with his right hand

2. Step forward with your left foot and grab the back of his right hand with your right hand.

3. Place your left forearm on his elbow and pivot your body 180 degrees.

4. Increase pressure to his elbow joint and drive him to the mat.

Pal-Kum-Chi 5

1. As your opponent grabs your sleeve with his right hand

2. Grab the back of his right hand with your right hand, and step forward with your left foot.

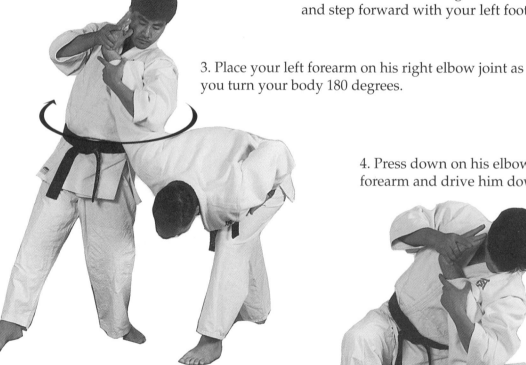

3. Place your left forearm on his right elbow joint as you turn your body 180 degrees.

4. Press down on his elbow joint with your left forearm and drive him down to the mat.

Pal-Kum-Chi 6

1. As your opponent grabs your right wrist with his right hand.

2. Step forward with your left foot and place your left forearm against his elbow joint.

3. Then step backwards with your right foot and turn your body 180 degrees. Deep step forward with your left foot as you push his right elbow joint with your left forearm.

Pal-Kum-Chi 7

1. Assume a fight stance.

2. As your opponent attacks you with his long stick, step backwards with your left foot and block the stick with your left hand.

3. Grab the middle of the stick with your right hand and pull him off balance.

6. Twist the stick out of his hands and assume a ready position.

5. Deep step forward with your right foot and push him into the mat.

4. Rotate your body 180 degrees as you push his left elbow joint with your right forearm.

Field Training - Washington State

SON-MOK-KUK-GI
손목꺾기

Son-Mok-Kuk-Gi 1

1. As your opponent grabs your right wrist with his right hand, open your hands (spread your fingers).

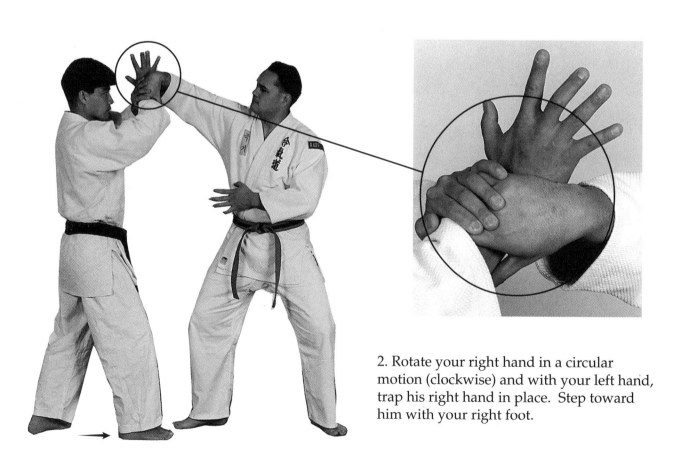

2. Rotate your right hand in a circular motion (clockwise) and with your left hand, trap his right hand in place. Step toward him with your right foot.

3. With a downward motion, drive him to the mat.

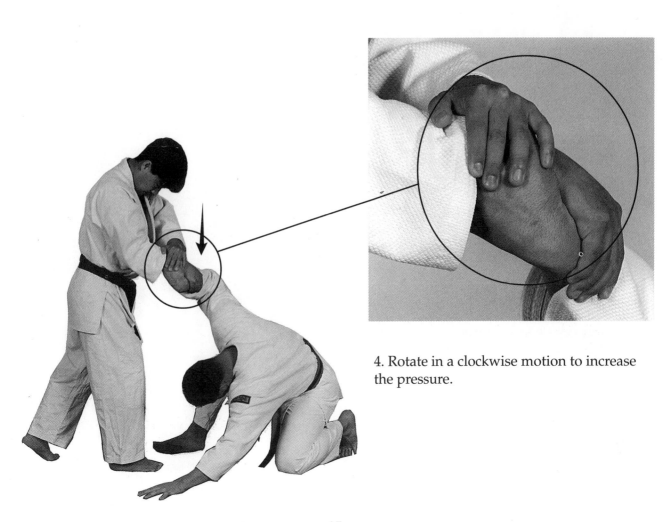

4. Rotate in a clockwise motion to increase the pressure.

Son-Mok-Kuk-Gi 2

1. As your opponent grabs your left wrist with his right hand, open your hands (spread your fingers).

2. Raise both of your hands together and step entering deeply towards him with your left foot.

3. With your right hand grab the back of his right hand and grab his right wrist with your left hand.

4. Step forward deeply with your left foot and drive him to the mat.

Son-Mok-Kuk-Gi 3

1. As your opponent grabs both of your wrists with both of his hand

2. Deep step forward with your left foot and rotate your left hand in a circular motion (clockwise). Grab the back of his right hand with your right hand.

3. Another deep step through in front of his body with your left foot. Free his right elbow joint with your left armpit. With a downward motion drive him to the mat.

Son-Mok-Kuk-Gi 4

1. As your opponent grabs your collars with his right hand

2. Grab his right hand with your right hand and grab his right wrist with your left hand.

3. Step forward with your left foot and bring your left elbow over his right arm.

4. Apply pressure to his wrist with your left arm and drive him to the mat.

Son-Mok-Kuk-Gi 5

1. As your opponent grabs your left sleeve with his right hand, open your hands (spread your fingers).

2. Grab his right hand with your right hand and with your left arm, rotate in a clockwise motion.

3. Place your left knife hand on the back of his forearm after you rotate his right wrist.

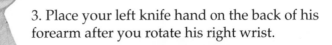

4. Deep step with your left foot and with a downward motion drive him to the mat.

Son-Mok-Kuk-Gi 6

1. As your opponent grabs your belt with his right hand

2. Grab his right hand with your right hand and place your left hand on his right wrist.

3. Deep step backwards with your right foot and turn your body 180 degrees in a clockwise motion.

4. Place your left knee on the back of his shoulder and pin him to the mat.

Son-Mok-Kuk-Gi 7

1. As your opponent grabs your right shoulder and right wrist from behind you.

2. Deep step forward with your left foot as you bend your right elbow.

3. Rotate your body 180 degrees in a clockwise motion as you rotate your right hand. With your left hand pin his right hand in place.

4. Slightly step forward with your left foot and with a downward motion push down on his wrist and drive him to the mat.

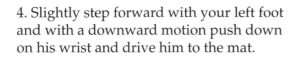

Son-Mok-Kuk-Gi 8

1. As your opponent grabs your right wrist with both of his hands

2. Step forward with your right foot. Rotate your right hand in a circular motion and with your left hand, trap his right hand in place.

3. Deep step forward with your right foot. Grab his right hand with your left hand and place your right knife hand on his right wrist. With a downward motion, push down on his wrist and sink him to the mat.

DUN-CHI-GI
던지기

Dun-Chi-Gi 1

1. When your opponent grabs your left wrist with his right hand

2. Step forward with your right foot and with your left hand grabs his right wrist. Place your right hand on the side of his face.

5. Rotate your body 180 degrees and place your right knee into his right shoulder. Thrust your right thumb downward into his throat.

4. Squat down and drive him to the mat.

3. Pulling his arm and pushing the side of his face. Step behind with your left foot. Turn your body 180 degrees and throw him off balance.

95

Dun-Chi-Gi 2

1. As your opponent grabs both of your collars with both of his hands

2. With your left hand grabs his left sleeve and grab his right upper collar with your right hand.

3. Kick his groin with your right foot (Instep groin kick)

6. After throwing him you can roll on top of him and punch his face.

5. Pull him towards you and with your right foot push him over you.

4. Lie back on the mat.

Dun-Chi-Gi 3

1. As your opponent grabs both of your collars with both of his hands

2. With your left hand grabs his left sleeve and grab his right upper collar with your right hand.

3. With your right leg sweep him to the mat as you thrust into his throat.

4. As you turn your body 180 degrees, place your right knee into his shoulder. Thrust into his neck with your right thumb.

Dun-Chi-Gi 4

1. As your opponent grabs both of your collars with both of his hands

2. Step forward with your right foot and place your left hand behind his head. Hold his chin with your right hand.

3. Step behind with your left foot. While twisting his head, rotate your body 180 degrees and throw him off balance.

4. Drive him to the mat and place your right knee into his shoulder, and twist his head.

Dun-Chi-Gi 5

1. When your opponent grabs your sleeves with both of his hands from behind you.

2. Step backwards with your left foot and raise your arms.

3. Step behind him with your right foot and throw him off balance with your right elbow.

4. Twist your upper body clockwise and drive him to the mat.

Dun-Chi-Gi 6

1. Deep step forward with your left foot and block your opponent's right punch with your left forearm.

2. Grab his wrist with your left hand and rotate in a clockwise motion. Then grab his hand with your right hand.

3. Step to the side with your left foot and place his arm over your shoulder.

4. Lean forward and throw him to the mat.

Dun-Chi-Gi 7

1. Deep step forward with your left foot and block your opponent's punch with your right hand.

2. Grab his wrist with your right hand and grab his sleeve with your left hand.

3. Deep step forward with your right foot

5. Throw him to the mat

4. Rotate your body 180 degrees
and pull down on his arm

Dun-Chi-Gi 8

1. Assume a ready position

2. Deep step forward with your left foot and block your opponents sword attack with your left hand.

3. Step to the side with your right foot and grab his left wrist with your right hand.

5. Throw him to the mat

4. Step back with your left foot and rotate your body 180 degrees.

Dun-Chi-Gi 9

1. Assume a ready position

2. Deep step forward with your left foot and block your opponent's stick attack with your left hand.

5. Throw him to the mat.

4. Rotate your body 180 degrees and lift the stick over his shoulder.

3. Deep step forward with your right foot and grab the stick with your right hand.

107

MOK-JO-RU-GI
목조르기

Mok-Jo-Ru-Gi 1

1. As your opponent grabs your right wrist with his right hand

2. Step behind him with your left foot and rotate your body 180 degrees. Place your left arm around his throat.

3. Step backward with your right foot and clasp your hands together. Pull him toward, you taking him off balance.

4. Drop to your right knee and place your left knee into his back and choke his neck.

Mok-Jo-Ru-Gi 2

1. Deep step forward with your left foot (45 degrees) as you block his right punch.

2. Grab his right wrist with your right hand as you turn your body 180 degrees and place your left arm around his neck.

3. Step backward with your left foot and clasp your hands together. Pull him towards you and take him off balance.

4. Lie back on the mat and wrap his legs with both of your legs and choke his neck.

HO-SHIN-SOOL
호신술

Kicking Defense 1

1. ROUNDHOUSE KICK - When your opponent kicks you with a right roundhouse, close in using a low block with your left hand and protect your face with your right hand.

2. Trap his leg with your left hand, placing your right hand on his shoulder. Take a deep step with your right leg and sweep him off balance.

3. Continuing in a circular motion, take him to the mat. Drop your right knee into his groin.

Kicking Defense 2

1. ROUNDHOUSE KICK - When your opponent kicks a right roundhouse, close in, block and trap his leg.

2. Take a step forward and as you twist his leg clockwise, sweep him off balance.

3. Drive him to the mat.

Kicking Defense 3

1. ROUNDHOUSE KICK - When your opponent kicks a right roundhouse, block and trap his leg.

2. Taking a step backwards, maintain pressure on his Achilles tendon

3. With a downward motion, pull him to the mat.

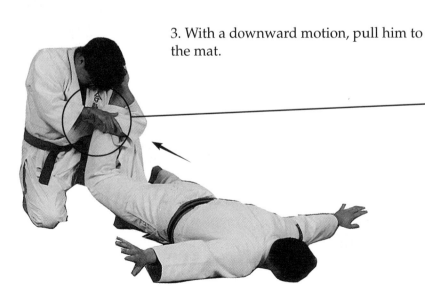

6. Shift your weight forward trapping his leg. Pull his hair and strike the back of his head.

5. Twist his foot creating pain

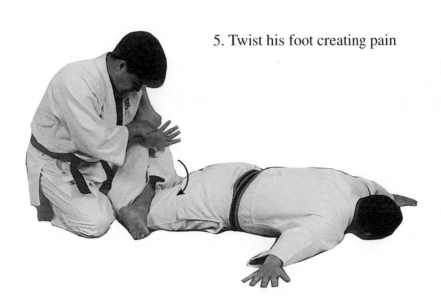

4. Wrap your left leg around his right leg. Grab his foot with booth hands.

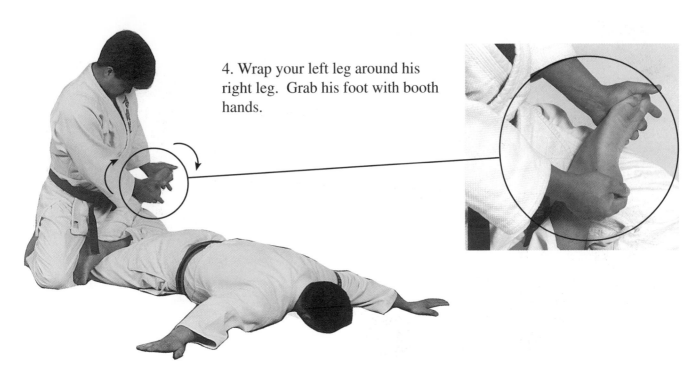

Kicking Defense 4

1. ROUNDHOUSE KICK - When your opponent kicks you with a right roundhouse, duck below his leg.

2. Circling to the right, sweep his leg with a sit-down spin kick

Kicking Defense 5

1. BACKSIDE KICK - When your opponent kicks you with his right backside kick, take a 45 degree step with your left foot. Block and trap his right leg.

2. Take a deep step with your right foot and sweep him off balance.

3. As he falls to the mat, trap his ankle with both hands and squeeze.

Kicking Defense 6

1. SPIN KICK - When your opponent does a right spin kick, take a 45 degree step to the right. Block and trap his leg.

2. Take a deep step with your left foot, stepping behind his foot.

3. Raise his leg throwing him off balance and forcing him to the mat.

Choking Defense 1

1. When your opponent has you in a headlock,

2. Grab his right wrist with your right hand and strike his left kidney with your left palm. Quickly remove your head and keep your grip on his right wrist.

3. Extend his right arm with your right hand and apply pressure to his elbow joint in a downward motion, and take him to the mat.

4. While he is on the mat, place your left knee on the back of his right shoulder. Apply pressure on his elbow while pulling up on his right wrist.

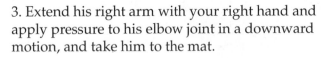

Choking Defense 2

1. When your opponent has you in a headlock, Wrap your arm around his waist and strike his groin with your right rear knife hand.

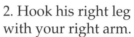

2. Hook his right leg with your right arm.

3. Lift him in the air.

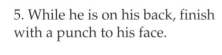

4. Continue to lift him as you turn to throw him on his back.

5. While he is on his back, finish with a punch to his face.

Choking Defense 3

1. When your opponent has you in a headlock while you are lying on your back

2. Grab his hair with your left hand as you grab his neck with your right hand pressing your thumb into his throat.

3. Kick your feet in the air and rock your body forward as you pull his hair and press on his neck, turning him on his back.

4. Turn your body upward while choking him and pulling his hair.

5. Lock your hands and press your left forearm on the side of his neck.

Choking Defense 4

1. When your opponent has you in a front headlock

2. Put your right arm around his head. With your left hand, grab your right wrist to lock his head.

3. Step back with your right foot as you pull down and begin to sit.

6. Finish by throwing him completely over.

5. As you lie on the mat, continue to take him over by lifting your right foot on his left leg.

4. Sit down and kick his left leg with your right sweeping kick.

Choking Defense 5

1. As your opponent has you in a headlock while your are lying on your back.

2. Pushing his head up with your left hand.

3. Slide your left foot up around his head. With pressure from your hand and foot, force him over

6. Put downward pressure on his elbow with both of your hands. Wrap your legs around his throat and choke him

5. Continue to choke him with your leg and put pressure against his elbow.

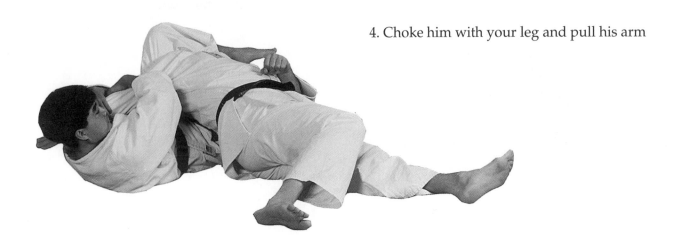

4. Choke him with your leg and pull his arm

125

Master Choe

YUN-KYEAL-GI-SOOL
연결기술

Pal-Kum-Chi / Son-Mok-Kuk-Gi

1. Your opponent grabs your right wrist.

2. Raise your right wrist and rotate it clockwise 180 degrees. Grab his elbow with your left hand and take a deep step forward with your right foot.

3. Step forward with your left foot and rotate your body 180 degrees.

7. Apply pressure to his wrist.

6. Deep step backwards with your left foot and rotate your body 180 degrees.

4. Grip his wrist with your right hand.

5. Bend his elbow and bend his wrist in a 90 degree angle.

Pal-Kum-Chi / Boo-Chae

1. Your opponent grabs your right wrist.

2. Deep step forwards with your left foot and rotate your body 180 degrees.

3. Step sideways with your right foot and twist your body 90 degrees

5. Deep step back with your left foot and rotate your body 90 degrees, driving him to the mat.

4. Step backwards with your right foot and twist his wrist 180 degrees.

Pal-Kum-Chi / Mok-Jo-Ru-Gi

1. Your opponent grabs your right wrist.

2. Step forward with your left foot and raise your wrist. Then rotate it 180 degrees.

3. Step back with your right foot and rotate your body 180 degrees,

5. Step back with your left foot and clasp your hands together and choke him.

4. Reach around his head with your left hand and place it under his chin.

Yun-Hang / Son-Mok-Kuk-Gi

1. Your opponent grabs your right wrist.

2. Grab his wrist with your left hand and step forward with your left foot.

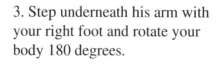

3. Step underneath his arm with your right foot and rotate your body 180 degrees.

7. Grab your wrist with your left hand and apply pressure to his bent wrist.

6. Place your right knee into his chest to pin him.

5. Place your left hand on his elbow and bring his right hand up and over his shoulder. Step forward with your right foot and rotate your body 180 degrees. Drive him to the mat.

4. Lift up on his wrist

Yun-Hang / Pal-Kum-Chi

1. Your opponent grabs your right wrist.

2. Grab his wrist with your left hand and raise his arm, then step forward with your left foot.

3. Step underneath his arm with your right foot and rotate your body 180 degrees.

6. Drive him into the mat. Then place your right knee on his elbow and apply pressure.

5. Step forward with your right foot and rotate your body 180 degrees.

4. Lift up on his wrist.

Yun-Hang / Mok-Jo-Ru-Gi

1. Your opponent grabs your right wrist.

2. Grab his wrist with your left hand and step forward with your left foot.

3. Step underneath his arm with your right foot and rotate your body 180 degrees.

6. Pull him towards you and choke him.

5. Reach around with your left hand and place it under his chin, then step back with your left foot.

4. Lift up on his wrist.

Son-Mok-Kuk-Gi / Pal-Kum-Chi

1. Your opponent grabs your right wrist.

2. Grab his hand with your left hand and rotate it clockwise 180 degrees then deep step forward with your right foot.

3. Push down on his wrist dropping him to his knees.

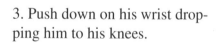

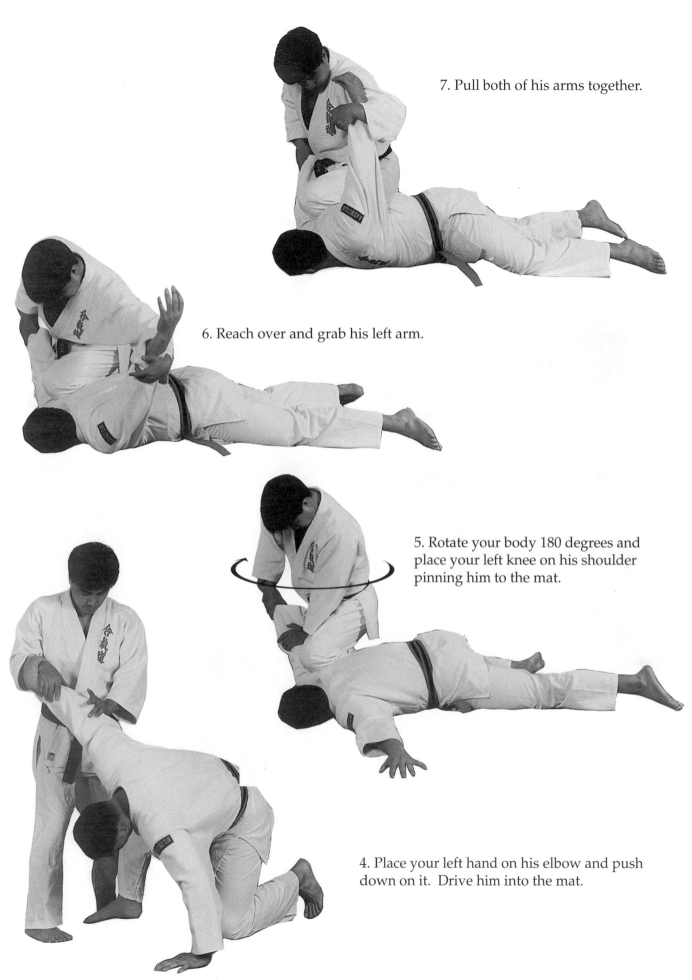

7. Pull both of his arms together.

6. Reach over and grab his left arm.

5. Rotate your body 180 degrees and place your left knee on his shoulder pinning him to the mat.

4. Place your left hand on his elbow and push down on it. Drive him into the mat.

Son-Mok-Kuk-Gi / Boo-Chae

1. Your opponent grabs your right wrist.

2. Grab his hand with your left hand and rotate it clockwise 180 degrees then deep step forward with your right foot.

3. Push down on his wrist dropping him to his knees.

7. Place your right foot under his arm and on top of his neck. Then rotate your body 180 degrees.

6. Rotate your body 180 degrees driving him to the mat.

5. Place your right hand on the back of his right hand then rotate his wrist counter clockwise.

4. Grab the back of his right hand with your left hand.

Son-Mok-Kuk-Gi / Hei-Jun

1. Your opponent grabs your right wrist.

2. Grab his hand with your left hand and rotate it clockwise 180 degrees then deep step forward with your right foot.

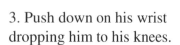

3. Push down on his wrist dropping him to his knees.

Please continue to next page for the last two steps ...

6. Step forward with your left foot and raise his arm in front of you.

5. Grab his wrist with your right hand and raise his arm upwards.

4. Grab the back of his right hand with your left hand.

145

7. Rotate your body 180 degrees and kneel down, then pull down on his hand and drive him into the mat.

8. Step forward with your left foot. Keep his wrist pinned to the ground with your right hand and push his elbow down with your left hand.

Son-Mok-Kuk-Gi / Boo-Chae

1. Your opponent grabs your right wrist.

2. Grab his hand with your left hand and rotate it clockwise 180 degrees then deep step forward with your right foot.

3. Push down on his wrist dropping him to his knees.

Please continue to next page for the next steps ...

6. Step forward with your right foot and rotate your body 180 degrees.

5. Step forward with your left foot and raise his wrist.

4. Grab the back of his hand with your left hand.

7. Step forward with your left foot and push down on his wrist.

8. Rotate your body 180 degrees. Place your left hand on the back of his right hand.

9. Grab the back of his hand with your right hand, then place your right knee on his shoulder and twist his wrist 90 degrees.

Master Choe

BAL-CHA-KI-SOOL

발차기술

Kicking Technique 1

1. Block your opponent's punch with your left hand.

2. Grab his right wrist with your left hand and kick his stomach with your right foot.

Kicking Technique 2

1. Duck down as your opponent punches.

2. Then kick his stomach with your right foot.

Kicking Technique 3

1. Block your opponent's punch with your left hand.

2. Grab his right wrist with your left hand and kick his stomach with your left foot.

3. Then place your left foot down on the ground and rotate your body 180 degrees.

4. Then kick backwards with your right foot and kick his stomach.

Kicking Technique 4

1. Block your opponent's punch with your left hand.

2. Grab his right wrist with your left hand and kick his groin with your right foot.

3. Then kick his head with your right foot.